The U.S. Army, Navy, and Air Force Medals of Honor (left to right) are unique in their design. Marine Corps and Coast Guard members receive the Navy medal.

Recipients of the Medal of Honor have distinguished themselves through "conspicuous gallantry and intrepidity" at the risk of their lives, "above and beyond the call of duty."

Congress created the Medal of Honor during the early years of the Civil War. Since then, about 3,500 individuals have been awarded the Medal of Honor.

Candidates are nominated by their commanders, and at least two eyewitnesses must attest to the candidate's actions. There is an extensive review and vetting process. When the honor is granted, the president bestows the medal in a ceremony at the White House. The award honors those who put aside their fear, and fight to preserve freedom and protect their fellow soldiers, airmen, seamen, and marines in all theaters of war—often against overwhelming odds.

THE MEDAL OF HONOR SERIES

by Michael P. Spradlin

JACK MONTGOMERY

World War II: Gallantry at Anzio

RYAN PITTS

Afghanistan: A Firefight in the Mountains of Wanat

LEO THORSNESS

Vietnam: Valor in the Sky

MEDAL OF HONOR

Leo Thorsness

MEDAL OF HONOR

Leo Thorsness
Vietnam: Valor in the Sky

MICHAEL P. SPRADLIN

FARRAR STRAUS GIROUX
NEW YORK

Farrar Straus Giroux Books for Young Readers
An imprint of Macmillan Publishing Group, LLC
120 Broadway, New York, NY 10271

mackids.com

Library of Congress Control Number: 2018955254
ISBN 978-1-250-15715-7 (hardcover) / ISBN 978-1-250-15713-3 (ebook)

Our books may be purchased in bulk for promotional, educational, or business
use. Please contact your local bookseller or Macmillan Corporate and
Premium Sales Department at (800) 221-7945, ext. 5442, or by email at
MacmillanSpecialMarkets@macmillan.com.

To the men and women of the U.S. military,
past and present, who keep our country free

CONTENTS

U.S. AIR FORCE RANKS

Partial list, from lowest to highest

Airman First Class
Senior Airman
Staff Sergeant
Master Sergeant
Second Lieutenant
First Lieutenant
Captain
Major
Lieutenant Colonel
Colonel

The ranks airman through master sergeant are noncommissioned officers. They are enlisted airmen who rose through the ranks and don't have a commission. Commissioned officers—second lieutenants on up—generally have a college degree. They are often graduates of a military academy or a university's Reserve Officers' Training Corps program.

MEDAL OF HONOR

Leo Thorsness

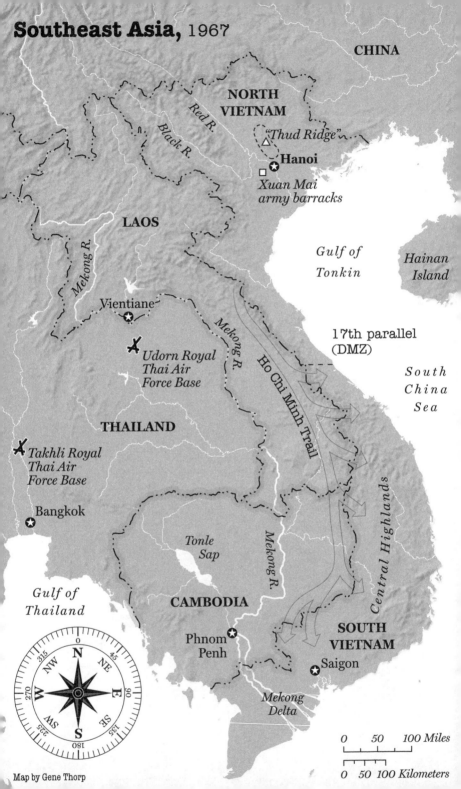

Southeast Asia, 1967

CHINA

NORTH VIETNAM

Red R.

Black R.

△ "Thud Ridge"

● Hanoi

□
Xuan Mai
army barracks

LAOS

Mekong R.

Gulf of
Tonkin

Hainan
Island

✪ Vientiane

Mekong R.

Ho Chi Minh Trail

17th parallel
(DMZ)

South
China
Sea

✈ Udorn Royal
Thai Air
Force Base

THAILAND

✈ Takhli Royal
Thai Air
Force Base

✪ Bangkok

Tonle
Sap

Mekong R.

Central Highlands

Gulf of
Thailand

CAMBODIA

✪ Phnom
Penh

SOUTH
VIETNAM

✪ Saigon

Mekong
Delta

Compass rose: N, NE, E, SE, S, SW, W, NW — 0, 45, 90, 135, 180, 225, 270, 315

0   50   100 Miles

0   50 100 Kilometers

Map by Gene Thorp

1
WILD WEASELS

WHEN COLONEL LEO THORSNESS, WHO THEN HELD THE rank of major, began his mission in Vietnam in the fall of 1966, he was undertaking a dangerous new form of aerial warfare. He was one of the Wild Weasels, a recently developed U.S. Air Force operation that had been code-named after the small but ferocious predator that will go to any length to attack its prey. Wild Weasels put themselves in extreme danger on every one of their missions to seek and destroy surface-to-air missile sites in North Vietnam. Provided

Uniform patch worn by the Wild Weasels

to the North Vietnamese Army by the Soviet Union, SAMs were becoming increasingly destructive to American aircraft.

Leading American strike forces into heavily defended airspace, the Weasels would troll around and entice the enemy to shoot at them. When the SAM operators took the bait and fired, the Weasels' own missiles would home in on the enemy radar and take out the site. The Weasels then had to avoid any incoming SAMs, which traveled at four thousand feet per second. As Thorsness remembered it, Weasel pilots would dive at top speed toward the ground, "and then at the last second . . . you'd haul back on the airplane as hard as you could," turning it skyward. "The missile couldn't make the corner with you. It would go under you and explode." It was the ultimate game of cat and mouse, and many Wild Weasel planes were shot down before they could achieve their objective.

As the "first in, last out," the Wild Weasels cleared a path for American bombers flying a few minutes behind to get in and get out, dropping their loads in relative safety. In Thorsness's words, "We would go in high enough to let somebody shoot at us and low enough to go down and get them; then we went in and got them."

An American F-105 trailing smoke after being intercepted by a surface-to-air missile. The missile was designed to detonate when it neared the target, scattering deadly fragments over a wide area.

In the early 1950s, jet fighters and bombers in the Korean War ushered in a new age of aircraft design and function. Ten years later, as American involvement in Vietnam intensified, the jet was commonplace and used in a variety of combat operations.

World War II had firmly established the importance of air support and controlling the sky in military conflicts. In the skies over North Vietnam, the United States sought to establish air superiority with jets, bombers, helicopters, and other aircraft. Jets were faster, more maneuverable, and able to carry far more ammunition and bombs than aircraft in earlier wars. Yet they were not invulnerable. Antiaircraft fire from tanks and other guns on the ground was still a danger, but the war in Vietnam brought the new threat of surface-to-air missiles. With

The Messerschmitt Me 262 became the world's first jet airplane used in combat when it attacked a British reconnaissance plane over Munich on July 25, 1944.

THE FIRST JET FIGHTERS

Leo Thorsness joined the U.S. Air Force only a dozen years after the first jet-powered airplane flew in Nazi Germany. Germans later flew the first jet fighters in combat, in 1944. The Messerschmitt Me 262 outperformed every other fighter plane in World War II, flying 120 mph faster than the American P-51 Mustang, but by that time, Germany was a year away from surrendering, and the new jet had little impact on the outcome. Allied attacks on factories, fuel depots, surface transportation, and airfields prevented the Germans from ever flying more than three hundred of the planes. Still, the German jet fighters shot down more than five hundred Allied aircraft, and Americans brought a few captured jets back to the States, where they influenced the design of the Sabre jets that flew in Korea.

This prototype of America's first jet-powered aircraft underwent test flights in California in 1942. The Bell P-59 Airacomet had a top speed of 450 mph and a range of 440 miles.

their radar-guided targeting systems and camouflaged launch sites, SAMs could appear out of nowhere and knock even the highest-flying jets out of the sky.

In 1966, to seek and destroy this new threat, Leo Thorsness and the Wild Weasels relied on the F-105 Thunderchief fighter-bomber. Pilots called it the Thud. "It was unwieldy and lumbering, but reliable with a strong heart," Thorsness said.

Bomb-laden F-105 Thunderchiefs heading toward enemy targets during the Vietnam War

THE THUD

The F-105 weighed over fifty thousand pounds, making it the heaviest combat fighter in history at the time. It could carry up to fourteen thousand pounds of bombs and missiles. Despite the weight, it was fast, cruising at 778 mph. With the afterburners, it could zip by at 1,390 mph. It also wielded a 20mm cannon. Its speed and complement of arms made it a lethal predator in Vietnam.

Thorsness had logged many hours in the Thunderchief by the time he reached Vietnam. He and other pilots loved it. The jet was tough and durable and—when the afterburners were lit—faster than enemy fighter planes.

The Thunderchief aircraft was initially designed in the 1950s to carry nuclear warheads very fast over great distances, as a defense against possible Soviet nuclear attack. But its use evolved over time. In Vietnam, the Thunderchief primarily dropped conventional bombs on North Vietnamese targets in Operation Rolling Thunder. As a bomber, the plane's main threats were antiaircraft weapons on the ground. But a dangerous enemy also lurked in the air. The North Vietnamese guarded the skies with Soviet-supplied MiG fighter jets. Not designed for aerial dogfights, the Thunderchiefs would have to outrun the MiGs until pilots developed tactics to use the Thud's speed and 20mm cannon effectively against the more nimble fighters.

Nearly all Wild Weasel missions were flown around Hanoi, the North Vietnamese capital. Thousands of antiaircraft guns and about 150 SAM launchers protected the region, along with a hundred MiGs on alert. General John P. McConnell, the air force chief of staff, called it "the greatest concentration of antiaircraft weapons that has ever been known in the history of defense in any town or any area in the world."

It was dangerous territory for Wild Weasels on the hunt.

THE UNITED STATES' WAR IN VIETNAM

IN 1857, FRANCE INVADED THE COUNTRY OF VIETNAM IN southeast Asia. French missionaries had been in Vietnam for centuries, trying to spread Catholicism among the Vietnamese. Like many other European nations, the French were eager to establish colonies around the world in areas that could produce raw materials for French industries and be a captive market for their products. It took many years for the French to subjugate the country. Vietnam eventually became part of the colony known as French Indochina, which also included the two kingdoms to the west, Laos and Cambodia.

With the end of World War II, citizens of countries

A depiction at Hoa Lo Prison Museum showing inhumane treatment by French colonialists of Vietnamese prisoners at the prison that would later be used by the North Vietnamese to hold American prisoners of war, who called it the Hanoi Hilton.

around the world began rebelling against their colonial rulers. This desire to rid themselves of European control of their governments and daily lives took root in India, Southeast Asia, and numerous countries in Africa. Vietnam was among the first. After living under French control for nearly seventy years and suffering a brutal Japanese occupation during the war, the people of Vietnam turned to communist Ho Chi Minh to fight for their independence.

Ho Chi Minh declared independence for Vietnam immediately after the Japanese surrender ended World War II in 1945, but world powers refused to recognize the country. They didn't want to anger their French ally, who was determined to keep its colony. War broke out.

Ho Chi Minh's communist-led independence movement was popular, and its forces waged a guerrilla campaign against the French. By 1950, they were receiving aid in their quest for independence from the communists who had just taken control of neighboring China.

Fearing another communist takeover in Asia, the United States began sending military advisers to Vietnam

THE DOMINO THEORY

Under presidents Truman, Eisenhower, Kennedy, and Johnson, the United States saw Vietnam and its communist-led independence movement as an example of the domino theory in action. Policy makers believed that once the first country in an area fell under the influence of communists, other countries would fall like a line of dominoes. After the communist takeover of China in 1949, the strongly anticommunist government of the United States wished to prevent any further expansion of the ideology in Asia.

Victorious Viet Minh troops loyal to Ho Chi Minh march into Hanoi in 1954.

in 1950 to assist the French in their fight against Ho Chi Minh.

In 1954, Vietnam and France, along with the United States, Soviet Union, China, and Great Britain, negotiated an end to the fighting. The Geneva Accords called for a cease-fire and temporarily divided the nation along the seventeenth parallel. France withdrew its military from communist-controlled North Vietnam and transferred its authority to a noncommunist regime in the South's capital of Saigon. The accords called for nationwide elections in two years to determine the future of Vietnam as a whole.

The elections were never held. Immediately, the

United States sent covert military operatives and economic aid to prop up the regime in Saigon. In October 1955, the South Vietnamese leader Ngo Dihn Diem declared himself president of the new, independent Republic of Vietnam. The United States endorsed this

U.S. military advisor (center) observing South Vietnamese troops, 1962

noncommunist ally and committed more economic and military aid to the new country.

Under President Dwight Eisenhower, U.S. involvement in Vietnam grew slowly, with about seven hundred military advisers in the country by 1961. Under the next president, John F. Kennedy, it increased quickly. Diem's corrupt regime was unpopular, and the communist Viet Cong had risen up in opposition. Kennedy began sending advisers to help Diem's army fight this threat, and by October 1963, there were sixteen thousand U.S. troops in the country. Yet no matter how many soldiers and advisers were sent, the South Vietnamese army remained ill-equipped to handle the Viet Cong.

On November 1, 1963, Diem was overthrown by his own army and executed a day later. This plunged South Vietnam into chaos. Three weeks later Kennedy was assassinated. Sensing an opportunity, communist leaders moved units of the North Vietnamese army into the South through Laos. Both China and the Soviet Union sent aid to support the offensive. Kennedy's successor, President Lyndon Johnson, committed even more military resources to Vietnam. By 1965, a full-scale war was under way.

In the fall of 1966, Major Leo Thorsness arrived in

Takhli Royal Thai Air Force Base, Thailand, April 1967. Several Republic F-105 Thunderchief aircraft can be seen on the ground.

Asia, attached to the 355th Tactical Fighter Wing of the U.S. Air Force. He was stationed at the Takhli Royal Thai Air Force Base in Thailand, an ally of the United States. Like all combat pilots in Vietnam, he was required to fly one hundred missions to complete his tour of duty and go home for good.

About halfway through his tour, Thorsness was able to travel back to his home base in Nevada on a short leave. As he remembered it in a 2002 interview, "When I went to Vietnam in 1966, it wasn't a big deal yet . . . The country didn't really know about that war, for a long time, so they didn't care."

Although antiwar protests had started on university campuses in the spring of 1965, the general public was slow to realize the scale of the United States' involvement in Vietnam.

"I went downtown and my wife went shopping, and I noticed people had no idea where Vietnam was. There was no more concern that we had people over there getting shot down every day than nothing, and people sat in prison camps."

Spring of 1965 antiwar protest in Philadelphia

North Vietnamese tanks crashing the gate of the presidential palace in South Vietnam, 1974, marking the end of the war

In the coming years the war would take up more and more of the daily newspaper headlines and nightly television news. It would become a very controversial war that would last for the United States until 1973. Supporters believed the war was necessary to stop the spread of communism. Opponents felt the war was a pointless waste of American money and lives.

By its end, over 58,000 U.S. military personnel would die. Up to 3.5 million more North and South Vietnamese civilians and military personnel would perish, as well as roughly 450,000 soldiers and citizens in Laos and Cambodia, the neighboring countries that were caught up in the long and tortured conflict. The war would finally end when North Vietnamese tanks crashed through the gates of the Presidential Palace in Saigon on April 30, 1975.

BOYHOOD

LEO THORSNESS WAS BORN NEAR WALNUT GROVE, IN southwestern Minnesota, on February 14, 1932. He was the youngest of three children, with an older brother and sister. Sixty years earlier, Walnut Grove had been a childhood home of Laura Ingalls Wilder. The fourth book in her famous Little House on the Prairie series, *On the Banks of Plum Creek*, is a fictionalized account of her family's struggles to establish a farm in the area. Like the Ingalls family, the Thorsness family were farmers.

It was the Great Depression—a time of severe economic struggle throughout the country. But with long hours of backbreaking work, "we defeated the

A 1937 painting of a Minnesota farm by Cameron Booth

Depression one day at a time," the future pilot said. "Later on I would discover that we had been poor—working hard to scratch out an existence. But we never went hungry." The family farm provided them with what they needed.

Living on a farm, Thorsness learned the value of ingenuity. His father bought a hay baler and converted a 1932 Chevy coupe into a tractor to pull it. Now they could bale their own hay and hire out to bale hay for neighboring farmers—"hard and itchy work," Thorsness recalled.

After graduating from high school in 1950, Thorsness enrolled in college at nearby South Dakota State University. In his first days there, he met Gaylee Anderson, whom he would marry within a few years. But after only one quarter, Thorsness decided he wasn't ready for the demands of college academics and that he was in need of some structure and direction in his life. In December 1950, with his older brother serving in the Korean War, he decided to put college on hold and enlist in the air force for a four-year stint.

Thorsness entered the air force because he "was serving without distinction in college," he later remembered. In the service he found a profession, not just a place to bide his time. After getting married and starting a

Leo Thorsness as a senior at Walnut Grove High School

Major Leo Thorsness and Captain Harry Johnson in early 1967

family, he wanted to get ahead and the air force provided all the opportunities he needed. Little did he know that seventeen years later he would still be in the air force, now a senior officer, flying highly dangerous missions in an altogether different war in Asia than the one in which his brother serverd.

With more and more missions in Vietnam under his belt, Thorsness became the most senior pilot among his fellow Weasels in the 357th, figuring out how to survive

MiG challenges and fifty-three surface-to-air missiles firing at him. He would experience white knuckles over the target area as "he nearly squeezed the control stick in two." And he would learn "the singular sensation of a flour-dry mouth in combat, when gum stuck to his teeth and to the roof of his mouth."

In his autobiography, *Surviving Hell*, Thorsness recalls that as a teenager in flight school he received what he considered invaluable advice from a fellow pilot who seemed to him a "crusty old aviator" because he was nearly thirty years old. The pilot told him that "there are old pilots and bold pilots, but there are no old, bold pilots"—a famous adage sometimes credited to E. Hamilton Lee, a pilot from the early days of the U.S. Air Mail Service.

The young Thorsness may have thought this was good advice, but on an April day long after his own thirtieth birthday, an "old and crusty" Major Leo Thorsness seemed to have put this advice aside and proved himself to be an extremely bold pilot indeed.

SAVING LIVES

ON HIS NINETY-FIRST MISSION IN VIETNAM, MAJOR
Thorsness and three fellow Thunderchief pilots were
given the assignment to destroy surface-to-air missile
sites at the Xuan Mai army compound not far from
Hanoi. North Vietnamese antiaircraft guns, SAMs, and
MiG fighters were lying in wait to engage the American
jets.

Major Thorsness would lead the four-plane flight,
call sign Kingfish, into Route Pack Six, the U.S. military's name for the bombing area around Hanoi. Sitting
behind him would be his "backseater" or "bear," Captain
Harry Johnson, the electronic warfare officer. As the

North Vietnamese SAM crew in front of a camouflaged missile launcher

EWO, Johnson was the eyes and ears of the two-man crew.

The Wild Weasels' two-seater Thuds were specially equipped to destroy the SAMs. They had antennas to pick up enemy radar, and it was the EWO's job to monitor threats on the plane's scopes and interpret the signals coming from below. A distinctive rattlesnake crackle in the headsets would alert the crew to an imminent missile launch as the SAM's radar locked on to the plane. Once a strong signal appeared on the Weasel's scopes, the EWO would direct the pilot to fire the Thud's Shrike missile, which would home in on the enemy radar and destroy the site.

Thorsness and Johnson had recently devised a new tactic for their Wild Weasel missions. Instead of approaching the target area as a group of four F-105s, they would split the flight into two and two. The SAMs had an effective range of about seventeen miles, and at this distance the SAM operators would have locked on to the incoming planes with their targeting radar. There would be little time to adjust to two moving targets as the Thuds flew within the seven-mile range of their own

A Thunderchief's cockpit

A SAM site viewed from the air

missiles. The strategy allowed the Weasels to attack two sites at once, but it was not without danger. With only two crews each to look out for enemy planes and surprise missiles, the separated Thunderchiefs could easily be overwhelmed. Still, the strategy would prove successful.

On this day, as the four planes approached the target, Thorsness sent Kingfish Three and Four to head north over the target area, while he and Kingfish Two flew to the south. A SAM locked on to their position, and with the guidance of his backseater, Johnson, Thorsness fired a missile, destroying the site.

But their euphoria was short lived. As often happens in combat, the mission took a bad turn.

Kingfish Three and Four were attacked by five MiG fighters. The MiGs had hidden themselves by flying at low altitude, making it difficult for the F-105s above to see them.

When Kingfish Three and Four attempted to outrun the slower North Vietnamese planes, one of the Thuds's afterburners—a part of the engine that gives the jet increased speed—failed to ignite. This forced them to withdraw and return to base. They were no match for five MiGs without their advantage in speed.

As Thorsness rolled in to take out a second SAM site with cluster bombs, the mission went from bad to worse.

North Vietnamese pilots and a MiG-17. Top speed 680 mph. Armaments: two 23mm cannons, one 37mm cannon.

BAILING OUT

Ejecting from a Thunderchief was dangerous. It was only done when the plane was too damaged to fly or when smoke filled the cockpit. Often the pilot did not have time to slow the plane down. At such high speeds the force of the airstream could cause severe injury as it yanked arms and legs into unnatural positions, or prevent ejection seats from propelling fliers cleanly away. The airmen could collide with the body or tail of the aircraft and be knocked unconscious. Unless they were physically capable of using the emergency radio they carried, there was no way to determine their condition.

A 2003 photo capturing the first moment of a pilot ejecting from his aircraft

"Kingfish Lead," came the call over the radio, "Kingfish Two is hit!"

Antiaircraft fire had hit his wingman. Thorsness instructed pilot Major Thomas M. Madison and EWO Major Thomas J. Sterling to head toward the hills in the west and keep transmitting so he could home in on them. He didn't know how badly damaged their Thunderchief was. Each minute they could stay in the air, moving away from the MiG-patrolled area, increased their chances of being safely rescued.

Over the radio—recordings of which are available online—came the beeping sound of the beacon that went off when a parachute opened. At least one of the men had ejected. The beacon did not indicate whether the flier was injured. Then came the beep of a second beacon. Both men had ejected. Their plane was going down.

Aboard Kingfish Lead both Thorsness and Johnson searched for the parachutes. Flying a jet fighter requires complex multitasking. The pilot's eyes flash quickly between the airspace and the dials and gauges, keeping track of fuel, speed, thrust, altitude, radio frequency— all while flying the aircraft, looking out for enemy fighters, and firing the weapons. Thorsness sharply banked the aircraft to fill the cockpit glass with the jungle below, a backdrop that made parachutes easier to spot.

"I have both chutes in sight, in the air," Johnson said from the back seat.

He had spotted the bright white parachutes about two miles ahead of them. Thorsness began circling the floating airmen to provide cover. If enemy planes spotted the parachutes, they would try to shoot the Americans down. Suddenly, Thorsness saw something in the corner of his eye.

"You've got a MiG, low!" Johnson had seen it, too.

In a matter of seconds, Major Thorsness had to make a life-or-death decision. His plane was the only friendly in the area. His wingman had been shot down and two fellow airmen were parachuting into enemy territory. He couldn't establish radio contact with either. The other two planes in his flight had already returned to base because of a faulty engine, and he was unsure if they had made it safely.

It was up to him to keep the airmen safe, even if he was running low on fuel and ammunition. Hopefully he wouldn't get himself and Johnson blown out of the sky in the process. Though his F-105 Thunderchief was not designed for aerial combat, Major Thorsness had no choice but to engage the enemy plane and protect the defenseless aviators. Thorsness was determined to defend the men of his squadron.

This particular MiG was a blunt-nosed MiG-17 with three cannons, two 23mm and one 37mm. It also carried Atoll heat-seeking missiles. Thorsness would have to be careful. This fighter jet could climb faster than a Thunderchief and was much more agile.

Thorsness maneuvered his Thud behind the MiG. It looked to him like he could reach out and pluck it from the sky. This plane was about to have a bad day.

"It appeared the MiG was going after the chutes so I took off after him. I was a little high, dropped down to about 1,000 feet, and headed north after him. We were doing about 550 knots and really catching up fast. At about 3,000 feet I fired a burst but missed. I lined him up again and was closing very fast. I was a bit below him now. At 700 feet or so I pulled my trigger and pulled the pipper [a part of the gun sight] through him. Parts of his left started coming off."

Thorsness had to put his aircraft into a steep dive to avoid colliding with the wreckage from the MiG.

"Suddenly I realized that Harry Johnson was frantically trying to get my attention. There were a couple of

A MiG-17 hit by a Thunderchief's 20mm cannon, June 1967

MiGs on our tail! If I had hit that MiG dead on, we probably would have swallowed some of his debris. But we got him. I lit the burner, dropped down as low as possible, and ducked into the hills west of Hanoi. The MiGs could not keep up with us."

Thorsness had destroyed one enemy fighter and duped two others into following him away from the downed pilots. He leveled his plane off and made contact with the HC-130 rescue-control aircraft covering the mission, call sign Brigham. He described what happened.

"Brigham Control, this is Kingfish Lead. Kingfish Two, an F-105F with two crew, is down," he said into the radio.

A C-130 testing helicopter-refueling capability, 1965

HC-130 HERCULES

The Crown Birds of Vietnam, HC-130s were used to coordinate search-and-rescue missions of downed personnel over both land and water. A variant of Lockheed's large and versatile C-130 transport plane, the HC-130 was equipped with a radio operator station, observation windows on each side of its fuselage, and an aerial tracker. Some C-130 aircraft were modified to refuel helicopters in flight, greatly extending the helicopters' range.

"Roger, Kingfish Lead, copy; Kingfish Two is down. Did you see parachutes?" Brigham asked.

"Affirmative, and two good beepers. Advise any rescue aircraft there are a bunch of MiGs around, and the location is in SAM range."

Thorsness needed to make another hard decision. He was critically short on fuel. He could not return to provide cover without refueling. But time was the enemy. It would take him ten minutes to reach the nearest airborne tanker. Another ten minutes to refuel. Then twenty minutes to return to the coordinates where he had last seen the parachutes. Brigham informed him that two rescue aircraft were already headed to the downed airmen's location.

He talked it over with Johnson. The rescue aircraft would be no match for the MiGs. Thorsness and Johnson agreed they would do whatever it took to give the two airmen on the ground the best chance at survival. They would refuel and return. "Hang in there, guys," Thorsness said to himself.

Thorsness pushed the throttle forward and the Thunderchief streaked through the sky, zooming faster than the speed of sound, toward the refueling tanker.

LEARNING THE ROPES

AFTER TWO YEARS IN THE AIR FORCE AS AN ENLISTED man, Thorsness enrolled in the Aviation Cadet Program. He and Gaylee married the same year he enrolled and had a daughter a year later, in 1954. Thorsness commenced his training at Lackland Air Force Base, in San Antonio, Texas. For fifteen months he and his fellow cadets were taught how to fly and how to become officers.

Thorsness remembered a challenging limbo period at the start of his training, when enlisted men thought he was putting on airs trying to become an officer—and officers were making it clear they thought the same thing. This didn't stop him from giving the training his all.

Then as now, becoming a fighter pilot in the U.S. Air Force is a rigorous process. Today, prospective pilots must train to be officers first. Then there's a year of what's called undergraduate pilot training, followed by six months to a year of advanced flight training on a specific aircraft.

Learning to fly modern jets tests pilots' physical and mental capacity to the limit. With today's advanced avionics systems, onboard computers, and satellite uplinks, many people think the plane "flies itself." Nothing could be further from the truth. Rather, modern jet fighters are so advanced that pilots must operate at the edge of human capabilities.

The g-force, or force of gravity, often causes air force trainees the most problems. Normal Earth gravity is 1g, the amount that keeps us walking on the ground instead of floating off into space. A force of 2g equals twice the earth's gravity, pulling us down, making us feel heavier, double our normal weight, and 3g equals three times the gravity, and so on. We feel g-forces when our bodies accelerate. In a commercial airliner, for example, passengers experience g-forces on takeoff, albeit only 1.1g to 1.3g. Modern fighter jets, on the other hand, are so fast, sleek, and maneuverable that pilots can experience up to 9gs—nine times the force of gravity—during certain maneuvers.

High g-forces make it difficult to move the arms and legs, which are obviously required to fly a jet aircraft, but high gs can also cause physical problems that endanger fliers' lives. When planes are twisting and turning in a dogfight, the blood in a pilot's body has a tendency to move away from the brain. This is especially true if the aircraft is in an upward vertical flight, upside down, or rolling. A lack of blood to the brain can cause a loss of consciousness.

Pilots undergo extensive training to counteract these effects. Prospective pilots are taught the Anti-G Straining Maneuver. They learn to anticipate a high-g move and clench their abdominal and leg muscles, pushing the blood into their arms, chest, and brain. As they clench, the fliers use a special breathing technique to maintain oxygen and decrease carbon dioxide in the blood.

Pilots practice this maneuver in a centrifuge on the ground. They sit in a pod that is spun around a room; the faster it spins, the higher the g-forces on their bodies. "G monsters" are the people who can maintain function at the highest gs.

Keeping as much blood in the brain as possible is vital. Of course, a pilot and his backseater are in grave

An Air Force centrifuge

danger if the pilot blacks out. Not only could it lead to an accident, but it could lead to defeat in aerial combat. In fact, there is a saying used in flight training: "Lose sight, lose the fight." Recordings from the cockpits of pilots engaged in combat or practice flights sound like a wrestling match. There are many grunts and groans as pilots navigate the high-*g* environment.

In the jet age, pilots like Thorsness developed tactics and strategies for aerial dogfights that are still used today. However, their planes—including the Thunderchief—were primitive compared to modern military aircraft. In addition, modern flight suits, called g-suits, are also designed to contribute to pilot performance. They are equipped with air bladders that automatically inflate and deflate, squeezing the legs, depending on the pilot's position at any given time. When inflated, the air bladders force blood from the lower extremities to the upper body.

Prospective pilots spend a great amount of time in the classroom, studying topics like physics and calculus, before they even get into a flight simulator. Once they begin flying, they have briefings every day before going up with a training officer in a two-seat training aircraft. As they advance through the training, they move on to more sophisticated planes.

When Leo Thorsness took his flight training at Goodfellow Air Force Base in San Angelo, Texas, he started with the L-21. The L-21 was a small two-seat Piper Cub aircraft. His first flight was taken with training officer Lieutenant Luellan, who taught him the basics, including the preflight inspection—walking around the aircraft to make sure there are no visible problems. "When the day for my first flight finally came, Lieutenant Luellan told me to grab my parachute and follow him. We walked across the ramp to the flying machines where he said, 'Follow me and watch what I check on the walk around.' After some explanation of what was important besides the fuel and oil levels, he said 'Okay, Thorsness, you fly from the front seat—try it on.' With eagerness and a bit of apprehension I climbed in, cramming my own bulk and that of my parachute into the tiny cockpit."

After flying with an instructor, Thorsness progressed to solo flights. He moved up to the T-6 Texan, a more advanced prop-driven aircraft that once trained World War II pilots. Then it was on to the T-28 and the T-33 jet trainer. Finally, Thorsness completed his training and received his wings.

By the end of the decade, Thorsness was assigned to Spangdahlem Air Base in West Germany, where he began flying his beloved Thunderchiefs. It was the height of

F-105s coming off the production line at a factory in Long Island, New York, early 1960s

the Cold War, and relations between the United States and the Soviet Union were tense. Both nations had built stockpiles of nuclear bombs and were prepared to use them if the other side attacked with theirs. During duty hours, Thorsness was stationed at the end of a runway with a nuclear warhead inside the bomb compartment of his F-105.

"We slept in concrete bunkers near the end of the runway so we could be airborne within 15 minutes if the 'bell went off.'" If the alarm sounded, it meant a nuclear attack was underway, and Thorsness's mission would be to deliver the warhead to a preselected target in Soviet territory.

During his time in Germany, he started taking night classes to continue his college education, and after his tour, he was given leave to finish his bachelor's degree at the University of Omaha before heading on to Nellis Air Force Base in Las Vegas, Nevada. While assigned to Nellis, he and his family lived in Los Angeles so Thorsness could earn a master's in aerospace operations management at the University of Southern California.

As nerve-racking as flying could sometimes be, he found that his engineering courses gave him literal nightmares. Luckily his wife was good at math and helped him, although he remembered that "most nights I stayed up until 2 or 3 a.m. memorizing formulas I didn't understand and math concepts I had never heard of."

Thorsness returned monthly to Nellis to fly enough hours to stay qualified on the F-105. After receiving his degree, he moved his family to Las Vegas.

His first day back on base he heard the news that would change his life forever. The operations officer welcomed him back, congratulating him on his degree. "And, by the way," he added, "this morning your assignment to Southeast Asia came in. You were at the top of the heap—lots of F-105 flying time and good gunnery and bombing scores. You are now a Wild Weasel."

RETURN TO ROUTE PACK SIX

THE FLYING TANKER WAS IN SIGHT. THE CLOCK WAS ticking. Kingfish Lead did not know if the crew of Kingfish Two was alive or dead.

Major Leo Thorsness was facing more than one enemy.

Refueling and flying back over North Vietnam to provide cover for his two downed airmen in Kingfish Two would put his own aircraft at grave risk. SAM sites and antiaircraft gunfire could shoot him down. Enemy MiGs, made for air-to-air combat, patrolled the sky. And he was down to his last few hundred rounds of

Thunderchiefs during a midair refueling run

ammunition. The tanker could provide fuel but not ammo.

The best option would be to act as a decoy, as he had done earlier, and get the MiGs to chase him. If he could trick the MiG pilots into thinking his Thunderchief was an easier target, they might turn their attention away from the crew of Kingfish Two and the incoming rescue aircraft.

Johnson, his electronic warfare officer in the back seat, would keep an eye out for enemy aircraft. Most of the time, two or more MiGs would slowly fly in a wide circle around an area, creating a wagon wheel with each plane at one of the "spokes," and wait for American planes to engage. But often they would make sneak attacks, using clouds and terrain to hide before dropping behind or above American planes to take them by surprise.

During his midair refueling, Thorsness learned from Brigham that two friendly A-1E Skyraiders, call sign Sandy, and a Huey helicopter were heading for the downed airmen's last-known position.

The search-and-rescue aircraft would reach the coordinates about ten minutes before the Thunderchief. While refueling, Thorsness radioed an alert to the search-and-rescue team.

"Sandy One, Kingfish Lead."

"Go ahead," replied the Sandy pilot.

"Sandy, be on your toes as you near the bailout area. There are MiGs in the area, and it's in SAM range."

"Kingfish, we copy that. Beeper plots to north twenty forty-one, east one-oh-five thirty-two."

"Roger that. SAMs can't handle low targets, so if you see a smoke trail, put it off one wing and take yourself down to the treetops. If you're looking at one [missile] when the smoke goes away, count to four, then pull hard toward the last place you saw it."

A-1E Skyraider

THE SPAD

A propeller-driven plane originally designed to bomb targets in difficult terrain, such as bridges in the mountains, the A-1E first saw combat in Korea. Well-armed with four 20mm cannons and sturdy, the Skyraider could fly a long time at low altitude, unlike jets, which required refueling. So in Vietnam the A-1E Skyraider, nicknamed Spad, was converted to search and rescue, used to fly over downed airmen and lay down fire to keep the enemy at bay until a helicopter could arrive to extract them.

"Sandy copies."

As the Thunderchief finished its in-flight refueling, Thorsness and Johnson had a brief conversation.

"Harry, if we go back, we go it alone." The odds were bad, but they agreed. They would return to help their friends.

As Kingfish Lead returned to the bailout area, they tried in vain to raise the crew on the radio. For a moment, they thought they heard a faint voice. But they couldn't be sure. And they could not verify if it was one of the crew. The North Vietnamese had become adept at using the radios taken from downed pilots to lure unsuspecting rescue aircraft. Sometimes, they even let the airmen run around in the jungle, thinking they were evading capture. A search-and-rescue aircraft would arrive only to meet a barrage of enemy fire. Retrieving downed aircrews was fraught with risk.

SAM radar started tracking their F-105, but they were still too far away for a launch. Kingfish Lead kept trying to raise Kingfish Two on the radio, hoping to hear any sign that the men were still alive and hadn't been captured. Thorsness was peering down at the green mountains when the situation turned grim.

"Leo, MiG eight o'clock!"

They had flown right into a wagon wheel. Like sharks around a sinking ship, four MiGs were circling the downed airmen.

Four.

Both men knew that the search-and-rescue team would never reach the pilots with MiGs waiting to blow them out of the sky. But Kingfish Lead had an advantage. None of the enemy planes had spotted him yet.

Thorsness dropped the Thunderchief down into the circle behind one of the MiGs and pulled the trigger on his guns. His last few rounds of ammunition ripped into the shiny metal skin. The MiG virtually disintegrated, spinning down into the green jungle canopy.

Thorsness rolled the Thunderchief into a dive and zoomed away from the other MiGs. Once out of range he keyed the microphone on his radio to call the rescue aircraft.

"Sandy One, this is Kingfish Lead," he said.

"Go," Sandy One replied.

"Kingfish One picked up a garbled transmission in the area. Might be one of the crew."

"Copy. Sandy's overhead now."

"Heads-up for MiGs. We just got another but there are at least three left."

Thorsness and Johnson tried again to raise the crew of Kingfish Two on the radio. There was no response. Frustration mounted. There was no more ammunition to take on the other MiGs, and fuel was running low yet again.

A frantic voice came over the radio.

"Sandy One is going in! Sandy One is going in—MiGs got 'em!"

Thorsness did not hesitate. The voice had to be coming from Sandy One's wingman.

"Sandy Two, get on the treetops! Get as low, slow as you can. Turn as hard as you can and the MiGs can't get you."

"Copy! I'll try!"

Thorsness dropped the Thunderchief's nose toward the trees and homed in on the harried Skyraider. Thorsness and Johnson spotted the MiGs almost immediately.

"MiG one o'clock," Thorsness said.

"And nine o'clock," Johnson said. "We're almost out of fuel," he added.

"They don't know that," Thorsness said.

"Another, seven o'clock," Johnson said.

Major Thorsness flew the Thunderchief into the middle of the MiGs like he was stepping into a hornet's nest. He dived at the enemy fighters, turning and climbing, using his speed advantage. The MiGs stopped their pursuit of the Skyraider and tried to bring their guns to bear on the whirling fighter plane challenging them.

Dipping, turning, and diving through the air, Thorsness was simply too skilled a pilot for the MiG pilots to match. Drawing them away from Sandy Two until it was able to get out of range, he left the MiGs behind and turned toward the tanker thirty minutes away.

On the Thunderchief's control panel, the fuel light blinked ominously.

THE DAY'S NOT OVER

MAJOR LEO THORSNESS AND CAPTAIN HARRY JOHNSON
had been flying for hours. They had shot down two
enemy planes and destroyed two different SAM sites.
Unknown to them, while they had engaged the MiGs
alone, Brigham Control had been desperately looking
for planes to come to their aid. They finally located a
flight of four Thunderchiefs, call sign Panda. The new-
comers engaged the MiGs and shot down two of them.

On Kingfish Lead's return to the refueling tanker, a
voice came over the radio.

"Leo, Panda Four here, I got six hundred pounds [of
fuel], am lost, can you help!"

South Vietnamese troops in search of the enemy on the Ho Chi Minh supply trail in Laos

Thorsness was shocked. Protocol required that personal names never be used over the airwaves in a combat area. During the dogfight, Panda Four had gotten lost. Now the plane was dangerously low on fuel.

"Tanker One, you have six minutes to rendezvous with Panda Four or he ejects. You gotta come farther north," Thorsness radioed in.

"Roger, Kingfish. We'll do our best," Tanker One responded. "And Panda Four, we are transmitting, home in on us."

Thorsness in Kingfish Lead and Panda Four were far apart, and the tanker could only take one of them. He and Johnson assessed the situation. "Even if we didn't get fuel, Harry and I agreed that we had a chance at making it to the Mekong River—the divide between Laos and Thailand—before flaming out. If we got past the Mekong, we could eject over friendly territory. But if Panda Four didn't refuel, he would have to eject over enemy territory. It was an easy choice: the tanker belonged to Panda," Thorsness said.

Torn apart by its own civil war between communists and forces supported by the U.S., Laos had been caught up in the American fight against the NVA and Viet Cong, and U.S. planes had been dropping bombs on enemy troops and NVA supply lines in the country for three years. It wouldn't be safe to bail out before the Mekong River. Kingfish Lead was 130 miles from Udorn, the nearest base in Thailand.

Thorsness took the Thunderchief up to thirty-five thousand feet to stretch the last bit of fuel. At the plane's best glide speed, 275 knots (310 mph), the Thud can glide for two miles for every thousand feet the slow speed will cause the plane to descend, so seventy miles from the Mekong River, Thorsness pulled the throttle back to idle. In fifteen minutes, they would glide over the river into Thailand. If they ran out of fuel, they could eject over friendly territory.

Finally, they spotted the Udorn runway, lined with emergency vehicles. They headed straight in and touched down. The engine quit as they rolled to a stop. They had made it.

"That was full day's work," Harry Johnson said.

"It was true," Thorsness would say later. "We had delivered our payload, shot down two enemy fighters [from] a plane not designed for aerial combat, kept our wingmen from getting murdered in their parachutes, and saved another U.S. aircraft. But as I retracted the canopy and stepped out of the plane, I felt like a failure, dejected at leaving two good men behind in the jungles of North Vietnam where they had probably been captured—or even worse—by now. If someone told me then that I would receive the Medal of Honor for this mission, I would not have believed him."

SHOT DOWN

ON APRIL 30, 1967, LESS THAN TWO WEEKS AFTER WHAT would become Major Thorsness's Medal of Honor mission, he and Captain Johnson attended a preflight briefing. The assignment that morning was to attack a supply depot near Hanoi. The Wild Weasels set out ahead of the strike force and destroyed a SAM site protecting the depot. They returned without incident. All twenty-four Thunderchiefs attached to the strike force made it home. After that mission, Thorsness and Harry Johnson had only eight more to go before they could return home to the United States.

The 355th Tactical Fighter Wing at Takhli had a rule

that aircrews flew only one mission a day. This was to avoid overtaxing the pilots, which could lead to fatigue-fueled mistakes. On each mission, two Thunderchiefs were held in reserve in case one of the assigned planes had to abort takeoff due to a maintenance issue.

On this day, there were no spare Wild Weasel crews available to stand in reserve. So Thorsness and Johnson returned to their plane and waited as a reserve plane, engines running, as the other aircraft lined up for take-off. The mission was set to hit a thermal power plant about thirty-five miles northwest of Hanoi. The target lay in the valley east of the infamous Thud Ridge, where many Thunderchiefs had met their demise in the Tam Dao mountains. The mission could be dicey, but if Thorsness and Johnson had to fly for some reason, they would knock off two missions in one day, leaving only seven more before they could go home.

As they waited for the planes to take off, one of the Weasels, call sign Carbine Three, had radio trouble and had to abort. So Major Thorsness and Captain Johnson took their position and taxied onto the runway. They took off with the rest of the Wild Weasels.

Approaching the target area, they could hear F-4 Phantoms ahead of them. The Phantoms were fighters designed specifically for aerial combat. They were sent to engage the MiGs guarding the SAM site. Inside Thorsness's plane, the air-to-air radar beeped in alarm. Something had locked on to one of them. Thorsness called the F-4 flight, call sign Cadillac, to see why they were getting a radar signal.

"Cadillac here, we've got air-to-air on us."

"Roger, I have you on our radar." Thorsness and Johnson assumed the F-4's radar systems were causing their alarms.

They were wrong. The radar signal was coming from two MiGs below them. The Thunderchief never stood a chance. As Thorsness and Johnson flew over, one of the MiGs fired an air-to-air missile. "We took one right up the tailpipe," Thorsness recalled. "It felt like we'd been smacked with a giant sledgehammer."

He immediately lost power to the controls, and the cockpit filled with black smoke. He got on the radio.

"This is Carbine Three. I've flamed out. Carbine Three flamed out. Mayday, Mayday, Mayday."

They were flying at 600 knots (nearly 700 mph). The maximum safe ejection speed from a Thud was 525 knots. But the plane could explode in the time it took to slow down. Thorsness and Johnson had discussed this scenario before. They would eject, no matter the airspeed, and take their chances.

"Go!" Thorsness shouted. Johnson had to eject first. If he waited, the rocket from Thorsness's seat would blast the rear cockpit with fire. Johnson's canopy blew, and his seat ejected.

Thorsness pulled his own handle and hurtled into the slipstream of his plane at 600 knots. "My helmet ripped off, my body felt as though it had been flung against a wall, and my legs flailed outward," he said. "Two seconds later, the chute opened, violently yanking me upward. My body rotated a couple of times, then settled into a float."

As he parachuted downward, he tried to assess the situation. When he had cleared the cockpit, the wind had snatched his lower legs and forced his knees sideways. His boots remained on, but the little pencil-sized zipper pockets on his jumpsuit sleeves were ripped off. "As I looked up at my chute I saw that at least a quarter of the panels were ripped open; I would be slamming into the ground faster than normal—with destroyed knees."

Off in the distance, he spotted Johnson's chute. Though he wasn't aware at the time, a MiG had also shot down his wingmen, Lieutenant Bob Abbott and his

A Thunderchief shot down over Hanoi, with pilot parachuting into enemy territory

backseater. Thorsness looked around and saw Thunderchiefs filling the skies. The strike force commander had canceled the strike and was organizing a rescue of the downed airmen. The planes roared by, coming within several hundred feet of the floating airmen, tracking them as they slowly spiraled down.

Thorsness pulled the emergency radio from the pocket on his parachute harness.

"Get me out of here!" he shouted.

They had ejected at ten thousand feet. That gave him several minutes before touching down. As Thorsness floated above the North Vietnamese jungle, he thought of his wife and daughter and what they might have to go through. His chances for rescue were slim.

He was still a few thousand feet in the air when something caught his eye. Muzzle flashes. They were shooting at him, he realized.

Thuds buzzed back and forth in the sky as he fell, crashing into the trees. He yanked to a stop roughly forty feet from the ground. His parachute had snagged on a branch. Next to him was a tall stand of bamboo, but he couldn't get a good enough grip to shimmy down. He spent ten valuable minutes working his way to the ground.

He had landed on the side of a mountain. Friendly planes continued to fly overhead, but he doubted they could spot him through the jungle canopy. He attempted another call on his emergency radio—but only heard garbled replies.

Thorsness could not stand. With each attempt his knees buckled and he crashed to the ground in agony.

A staged North Vietnamese propaganda photograph of a citizen capturing a U.S. pilot

He heard voices down the hill and started crawling on his hands and knees, trying to find a clearing. If the Thuds could see him, they could use their guns to drive back his pursuers until a helicopter could rescue him.

His injuries slowed him down. The enemy was gaining. Thorsness heard their shouts as they approached.

"I rolled on my back to face them. There were a dozen or more: all young males, maybe 15–20 years old. Most were armed with machetes. I saw one real rifle, an old one, and a couple wooden rifles, probably for training. They grabbed my feet and arms, and sat me upright. One pulled out a black cloth bag—pillow-case size. The last thing I saw just before he slipped it over my head was the hate-filled eyes of a young Vietnamese pulling back a machete to strike me."

Major Leo Thorsness's final flight of the Vietnam War had come to a horrible end.

POWS

DURING THE AMERICAN CONFLICT IN VIETNAM, AT least 766 U.S. service members were captured and held as prisoners of war by the North Vietnamese. The largest percentage of captives were aviators in the U.S. Air Force and Navy. Shot down over North Vietnam, they were kept in a network of prisons, mainly around the capital of Hanoi. Many ended up at the infamous Hoa Lo Prison, which captives nicknamed the Hanoi Hilton.

In 1965, the North Vietnamese army began a program of systematic torture of U.S. POWs. Beatings and sleep deprivation were common forms of abuse. Prisoners were chained by the ankles to concrete slabs for hours at a time, allowing them little to no movement. They were given scant food and seldom allowed to bathe.

The North Vietnamese used the POWs as leverage in peace negotiations. They often attempted to get prisoners to make recordings condemning the war. Many refused. Commander James Stockdale, a naval aviator, slit his own scalp with a razor and smashed his face with a stool, which left him so bruised and bloody that the North Vietnamese were unable to film him for propaganda. Stockdale even went so far as to slash his own wrists to

A North Vietnamese propaganda photograph showing POWs receiving plentiful food. In reality, prisoners were poorly fed.

Lieutenant Commander John S. McCain (center) being captured by Vietnamese civilians near Hanoi, Vietnam, 1967

show he'd rather die than submit to torture. He was later awarded a Medal of Honor for his actions as a prisoner.

Some prisoners made the recordings but used subtle gestures and facial expressions unfamiliar to the Vietnamese. They hoped that the U.S. military would see the deception and realize they were being tortured and coerced. Many countries condemned North Vietnam for its treatment of prisoners. Yet despite the outcry from the international community, the torture continued.

Another POW, Lieutenant Commander John S. McCain III, was held captive for almost six years after he was shot down. He later became a senator from Arizona and a 2008 candidate for president. McCain's father, Admiral John S. McCain Jr., was an outspoken foe of communism who became commander in chief of all U.S. forces in the Pacific in 1968. The North Vietnamese felt they had captured a prize in the young McCain and offered to send the naval aviator home as part of a goodwill propaganda gesture. McCain repeatedly refused. They ended up torturing him for more than a year, rebreaking an arm that had recently healed after his crash.

Prisoners were moved from location to location, and many were kept in solitary confinement for years at a time. The North Vietnamese did not want prisoners to talk to each other, but the prisoners devised a method of communicating between cells. It was dangerous and took extreme caution. If a POW was caught even attempting to communicate with a comrade, he was severely punished.

The communication method was a tap code.

Military prisoners as far back as ancient Greece have used tap codes, and the POWs in the Vietnam War used theirs extensively. They were able to send messages back

SECRET COMMUNICATION

The tap code used a series of taps that corre-
sponded with letters laid out on a grid. There were
five rows of five letters each. The letter *K* was
excluded and the *C* was used instead. The letter *X*
was used to separate sentences.

The grid looked like this:

TAPS	1	2	3	4	5
1	A	B	C	D	E
2	F	G	H	I	J
3	L	M	N	O	P
4	Q	R	S	T	U
5	V	W	X	Y	Z

First you would tap the row number, then after
a quick pause you would tap the letter. So, for
example, *boy* would be spelled as follows: one
tap, two taps; three taps, four taps; five taps, four
taps. To make it easier, the POWs created short
words and acronyms for common words and
phrases. GBU stood for *God bless you*. YS stood
for *Yes, sir*.

and forth regarding the health of other prisoners. They would use it to make up stories that they could "reveal" under torture. The code allowed everyone to know the fake intelligence they were passing along so they could deceive their captors.

The tap code allowed the prisoners to maintain some semblance of military order. Many prisoners credit the tap code with keeping them sane in a truly horrific situation. They were able to keep up on news and maintain the basic human contact they needed to survive, even when they were isolated and alone. Some prisoners were so adept at the code that they could sit next to each other, ordered by the guards not to talk, and tap out messages on each other's thighs without the guards noticing.

CAPTURED

SURROUNDED BY YOUNG ENEMY FIGHTERS, THORSNESS lay on the jungle floor waiting for a killing blow from the raised machete he'd seen before a bag was pulled over his head. The blow never came. They removed the bag and tried to force him to stand. Each time, he collapsed on broken knees. They insisted that he walk, but each step sent him tumbling to the ground. No matter how hard they beat him, he could not walk.

Using gestures, Thorsness attempted to explain to his captors that he wanted to use bamboo to construct splints for both his legs above and below his damaged knees. "They split the bamboo. Eventually four took belts from their pants and I used them to tie the bamboo to my legs. Of course, the strips cut into my knees and legs, and stayed in place just a few steps. After a couple of tries, my body and mind gave out." Thorsness fell unconscious.

He woke up later being carried in a large net the youths had attached to two poles. In this sling, they carried him down the mountain to a large shack. It was full of older men. His backseater Harry Johnson was there, tied up. Thorsness was shoved to the ground beside him and tied in the same manner. Both men were beaten and bloody. Whenever the two attempted to speak to each other, they were hit.

Thorsness believed the old men would decide their fate. Risking a beating, he told Johnson, "Harry, I think this is a trial, and we may be executed tonight."

"Leo, either they will or won't, we can't control it. No sense worrying about it," Johnson replied.

Thorsness was in relentless pain. Their captors left them on the floor, and they slept fitfully that night. The next morning, they were moved to a small building in the foothills and locked in separate rooms. Thorsness soon fell asleep but awoke when he heard his friend and fellow officer being taken out of his cell.

"Fifteen minutes later I heard him stumble back into

his room. Then there was a jingling of keys—a sound that would soon take on sinister implications—and my door opened. They let me use sticks for support as I dragged myself out. As I passed Harry's door, he hollered, 'Geneva Convention, Leo. Hold out.' I shouted back: 'Do my best.'"

The interrogations had begun.

The international community put pressure on North Vietnam to obey the Geneva Conventions. Publicly, North Vietnam claimed to be treating the POWs humanely. But in reality, the prisoners suffered horribly.

As Leo Thorsness was taken to his first interrogation, he steeled himself to reveal nothing but what the Geneva Convention required. The method used to extract information was unusual, to say the least. He was tossed into a pig pen filled with dirty muck and pigs rooting in the muddy soil. He was asked about targets and missions, and each time he answered with his name, rank, serial number, and date of birth. He was beaten with a stick for refusing to answer, but he made it through the first session.

That night, Thorsness was loaded into the back of a military truck. His captors forced him onto his back. Thorsness stretched his arms in the dark vehicle and felt

Geneva Convention identification card given to U.S. military personnel

THE GENEVA CONVENTIONS

The Geneva Conventions are international treaties and protocols that protect noncombatants in war, such as civilians and the sick and wounded. The Third Geneva Convention specifically governs how prisoners of war are supposed to be treated. It requires that they be given adequate food and shelter and be treated for wounds or injuries. It states that prisoners are only required to reveal four pieces of information: name, rank, date of birth, and serial number. It prohibits torture or any other coercion to compel them to provide more than that.

However, several countries do not recognize

the Geneva Conventions. The Japanese did not follow them in World War II. North Vietnam saw the war as an illegal act of aggression by the United States and deemed the prisoners "war criminals" not protected by the protocols. The prisoners were beaten and starved and given little to no medical treatment.

the edge of the truck bed on one side, and another body to his right.

"Is that you, Harry?" he asked.

"It's me, Leo," Johnson replied.

A guard shouted and hit them both.

Each jolt along the bumpy roads brought pain. Any time Thorsness tried to make himself comfortable, he was whacked with a club and forced to lie in the same position. Finally, they reached a paved road and eventually turned off and stopped. The truck backed up, and they were unloaded.

They had arrived at the infamous Hoa Lo Prison. The Hanoi Hilton.

After ninety-two and a half missions together, that was the end of direct contact between the pilot and his backseater for six years. "Harry and I were dragged out of the back of the vehicle and separated. It would be three years before I got a glimpse of Harry again across the prison yard—the guard opened my cell door a couple seconds before Harry was back inside his cell." It would be three more years before he would have a chance to talk to Johnson again.

Entrance to the Hanoi Hilton prison

11
SIX LONG YEARS

FOR THE NEXT SIX YEARS, LEO THORSNESS AND THE REST of the POWs endured unimaginable hardships. Interrogation started immediately upon his arrival at the Hanoi Hilton.

"The setting was ominous. The walls in the small room where they put me were knobby with hand-daubed concrete. (It hurts a lot more when you are knocked against knobs than against smooth walls.)"

The interrogators sat behind a narrow table, staring down intimidatingly as Thorsness sat on a short wooden stool in front of them.

"The questions came like anti-aircraft flak. What was your target? What is the target tomorrow? Who is your squadron commander? What is your wife's name? I gave the Geneva Convention answer. That didn't work. One of the guards hit me in the head and knocked me off the stool."

Thorsness was forced to lean headfirst against the knobby wall as the guards beat him. He was jerked around the room by his hair. His arms were bound and yanked behind his back until his elbows touched and his shoulders dislocated. His back was broken several times.

Session after session, he was tortured and abused. Finally, he came to understand that it was not really information the North Vietnamese desired. They wanted the American prisoners to condemn the war and admit they were war criminals. They would torture and abuse prisoners until they were broken and force them to sign confessions.

"Each of us had a different threshold of pain. Each reached the breaking point in a different moment. The rule old-hands tried to pass to new prisoners as quickly as possible was this: 'You cannot give information because of verbal abuse. You must take physical punishment until you are on the verge of losing your mental capacity to be rational. When you reach that point: lie,

An air force captain navigating with a compass for her team during SERE training

cheat, and do whatever you have to do to stay sane. Whatever lies you tell, keep them simple so you can remember them.'"

The U.S. military has since devoted numerous resources to understanding how service members react to capture and torture. Since most aviators have a high chance of being shot down behind enemy lines, they undergo extensive training in SERE—survival, evasion, resistance, and escape.

Military personnel are trained to resist torture and interrogation.

Military leadership devoted more time to training in

THE MILITARY CODE OF CONDUCT

Each service member is expected to follow the six articles of the Code of Conduct for Members of the United States Armed Forces:

I. I am an American, fighting in the forces which guard my country and our way of life. I am prepared to give my life in their defense.

II. I will never surrender of my own free will. If in command, I will never surrender the members of my command while they still have the means to resist.

III. If I am captured I will continue to resist by all means available. I will make every effort to escape and aid others to escape. I will accept neither parole nor special favors from the enemy.

IV. If I become a prisoner of war, I will keep faith with my fellow prisoners. I will give no information or take part in any action which might be harmful to my comrades. If I am senior, I will take command. If not, I will obey the lawful orders of those appointed over me and will back them up in every way.

V. When questioned, should I become a prisoner of war, I am required to give name, rank, service number, and date of birth. I will evade answering further questions to the utmost of my ability. I will make no oral or written

> statements disloyal to my country and its allies
> or harmful to their cause.
> VI. I will never forget that I am an American, fight-
> ing for freedom, responsible for my actions,
> and dedicated to the principles which made
> my country free. I will trust in my God and in
> the United States of America.

resistance techniques after the Korean War. Prisoners in Korea were horribly tortured, some of them unable to recover. This caused the United States to rethink its training policy prior to sending troops into combat. What came to be understood is that even the strongest will break eventually.

Leo Thorsness lasted eighteen days before he gave up information beyond what was required by the Geneva Conventions.

"When I broke—when I went beyond name, rank, serial number, and date of birth—it was the lowest point in all my six years of captivity."

When he was taken from solitary confinement, he was placed in a cell with two other prisoners, Ev South-wick and Jim Hiteshew. Hiteshew had been so severely injured ejecting from his plane—two broken legs and a broken arm—that the North Vietnamese had placed him in a primitive body cast.

Overcome with guilt, Thorsness confessed that he had failed to withstand the torture of his captors. The injured pilot gruffly told him to knock it off.

"Don't you know?"

"Know what?" Thorsness asked.

"That everyone who goes through that type of interrogation has one of two things happen: either they broke or died—some did both."

This was exactly what the demoralized pilot needed to hear. "There was—and there still is—no way for me to express my absolute euphoria at hearing those words. I was not a failure. I was average and happy to be so."

The six years Thorsness spent in captivity were marked by sickness and depression, yet incredible acts of courage and endurance. For the first three years, the prisoners were isolated for the most part. Still, using the tap code and other methods, the prisoners managed to maintain a chain of command and keep one another's spirits up as best they could.

In October 1969 the policy changed toward prisoners. Torture and interrogation lessened for those who had been in captivity for years. They were grouped together, and this greatly improved their spirits. They held church services. Those who had expert knowledge in certain academic disciplines taught classes. All these activities were important in helping prisoners maintain human connections and boost morale.

The prisoners always tried to find ways to undermine the guards and subvert their authority. In one case, they managed to smuggle peppers to their cells from a wild pepper plant growing in the prison yard. Moments like this were tiny victories; the effect on morale was enormous.

The peppers were a welcome addition to a prison diet of almost exclusively rice, with very little protein. Before long, most of the prisoners were physical shadows of their former selves. Thorsness estimates that due to poor nutrition in prison he lost at least forty pounds, weighing as little as 135 pounds during captivity.

From acting out movies to memorizing poetry, the prisoners found creative ways to keep their minds intact and maintain their sanity. Many of them were broken in body and spirit, but when they were finally grouped together, they were able to help each other keep going and not lose hope.

Once Leo Thorsness was brought to the Hanoi Hilton, it took him a long while to recover from the injuries he had sustained in ejecting from his Thunderchief, not to mention the injuries inflicted by being tortured repeatedly during his first days and weeks in captivity.

During his confinement, Thorsness was moved to different prisons within the North Vietnamese system. In the summer of 1969, two years into his captivity, Major Leo Thorsness received an astonishing message by tap code: LT U NOMINATED 4 MOH.

So it was that this Wild Weasel learned he had been nominated for the Medal of Honor for his heroic actions on April 19, 1967, eleven days before being taken prisoner—that extraordinary Wednesday when he kept his wingmen alive, shot down two MiGs, gave up his chance to refuel to save another pilot, and still eked out a safe return for himself and his backseater.

Thorsness learned of the nomination from pilot Jim Clements, who was shot down six months after Thorsness and ended up in the same Hanoi prison. Clements had flown Thuds out of Takhli and had learned

The plane flown by Thorsness on his Medal of Honor mission

that Bill Sparks, one of Thorsness's fellow Wild Weasels, was doing the research required to recommend him for the medal.

Word of Thorsness's nomination spread through the prison. But the news was kept secret from their captors. The North Vietnamese were particularly brutal to pilots, whom they held responsible for wreaking so much havoc on their country. If they learned that Thorsness would be awarded a Medal of Honor for his actions, they would have singled him out for especially horrific torture. The United States

Air Force also knew this and kept the news from the American public.

But across the world in the Hanoi Hilton, the news of his Medal of Honor was a tremendous morale boost for every captive.

HOME 12.

LEO THORSNESS WAS A CAPTIVE OF THE NORTH VIET-
namese for nearly six years. In January 1973, the United
States and North Vietnam signed peace accords in Paris
ending U.S. military action in Vietnam. As part of the
treaty, North Vietnam agreed to release all current
POWs. In the weeks before their release, the prisoners
started to receive better food and medical treatment.
The North Vietnamese did not want the world to see
beaten, emaciated men when they were released.

At first the men did not believe the improved con-
ditions meant freedom was near. They thought it was
another cruel trick, perpetrated by the North Vietnamese

to further torture them psychologically. They assumed the improved food would be given to them for a short time, then yanked away as soon as they grew used to it. But it was no trick. They were, at last, going home.

The prisoners were released in stages. They were given gray coveralls and bused to the airport, where they boarded a C-141 transport plane. Many still could not believe they were free. It wasn't until the airplane lifted off that they let out a cheer. Many of them sobbed in relief at the end of their long ordeal.

Operation Homecoming carried home prisoners for two months. Leo Thorsness was flown out March 4,

POWs homeward bound on board an air force C-141

along with his backseater Harry Johnson and his downed wingmen Tom Madison, Tom Sterling, and Bob Abbott.

On their stop in the Philippines, Thorsness was able to call home.

"Gaylee," he said, "I would have called sooner but I've been all tied up."

Six days later at Scott Air Force Base near St. Louis, he was finally reunited with his family.

It took three operations to repair his injured knees and back. While still recovering he was taken to the

President Richard M. Nixon presents the Medal of Honor to now-Colonel Leo Thorsness

White House, where on October 15, 1973, President Richard Nixon formally presented him with the Medal of Honor for his mission over North Vietnam. As he stood there on his crutches, he was thinking, "Why me? I'm so average. There were people who deserved as much or more and were braver."

Promoted to colonel, Leo Thorsness was given a medical discharge from the air force. A long, honorable, and difficult chapter of his life had come to a close. But Colonel Thorsness was not through serving his country.

Leo Thorsness entered politics. In 1974, he ran against former presidential candidate George McGovern for U.S. senator of South Dakota and lost by a narrow margin. Eventually, he moved to the state of Washington and served a term in the state senate. After serving his term, Colonel Thorsness finally retired for good.

In 1993, Thorsness and his wife, Gaylee, returned to Hanoi. He toured the Hoa Lo Prison, which is now a museum. Many POWs have returned to Hanoi, in an effort to bring closure to one of the most horrific experiences of their lives.

In a 2002 interview, Thorsness was asked what lessons he hoped young people might take from his Medal

Thorsness speaking at an Air Force Association conference in 2010

of Honor. Thorsness replied, "Well, I would hope the kids today, if they look at it now or at some distance out, that they understand how important freedom is . . . I didn't appreciate it until it was taken from me, and I don't know that anyone can until they've lost it . . . If you let it slip away very long, it's gone. And I would hope that they would learn that from these kinds of experiences that leaders are made, they're not born. That you can come from any walk of life and become a leader and that one person can make a difference. It doesn't matter what your status is . . . Not so long ago, I designed a medallion, a coin. On the one side it says *freedom*. And I said what word is the flip side of *freedom*? And I finally came up with it—it's *responsibility*. If every one of us will accept our responsibilities as best we can, we can go on forever."

Leo Thorsness passed away on May 2, 2017. But the memory of his deeds will carry on.

LEO K. THORSNESS'S MEDAL OF HONOR CITATION

THE PRESIDENT OF THE UNITED STATES
IN THE NAME OF THE CONGRESS TAKES
PRIDE IN PRESENTING

THE MEDAL OF HONOR

TO LIEUTENANT COLONEL LEO K. THORSNESS,
UNITED STATES AIR FORCE

FOR SERVICE AS SET FORTH IN THE FOLLOWING CITATION:

For conspicuous gallantry and intrepidity in action at the risk of his life above and beyond the call of duty. As pilot of an F-105 aircraft, Lt. Col. Thorsness was on a surface-to-air missile suppression mission over North Vietnam. Lt. Col. Thorsness and his wingman attacked and silenced a surface-to-air missile site with air-to-ground missiles and then destroyed a second surface-to-air missile site with bombs. In the attack on the second missile site, Lt. Col. Thorsness' wingman was shot down by intensive antiaircraft fire, and the 2 crewmembers abandoned their aircraft. Lt. Col. Thorsness circled the descending parachutes to keep the crewmembers in sight and relay their position to the Search and Rescue Center. During this maneuver, a MIG-17 was sighted in the area. Lt. Col. Thorsness immediately initiated an attack and destroyed the MIG. Because his aircraft was low on fuel, he was forced to depart the area in search of a tanker. Upon being advised that 2 helicopters were orbiting over the downed crew's position and that there were hostile MIGs in the area posing a serious threat to the helicopters, Lt. Col. Thorsness, despite his low fuel condition, decided to return alone through a hostile environment of surface-to-air missile and antiaircraft defenses to the downed crew's position. As he approached the area, he spotted 4 MIG-17 aircraft and immediately initiated an attack on the MIGs, damaging one and driving the others away from the rescue scene. When it became apparent that an aircraft in the area was critically low on fuel and the crew would have to abandon the aircraft unless they could reach a tanker, Lt. Col. Thorsness, although critically short on fuel himself, helped to avert further possible loss of life and a friendly aircraft by recovering at a forward operating base, thus allowing the aircraft in emergency fuel condition to refuel safely. Lt. Col. Thorsness' extraordinary heroism, self-sacrifice, and personal bravery involving conspicuous risk of life were in the highest traditions of the military service, and have reflected great credit upon himself and the U.S. Air Force.

KEY TERMS

afterburner A device in the tailpipe of a jet engine that injects fuel into the hot exhaust gases and burns it to provide extra thrust. It gives the jet a sudden and powerful burst of speed but consumes a lot of fuel and is used only when necessary.

Cold War The rivalry between the United States and the Soviet Union, along with their respective allies, that developed as each tried to protect its interests after World War II.

communism A political system where the government controls all property and resources, allocating their use based on its determination of the people's needs.

EWO or **electronic warfare officer** An officer trained in the electronics of the aircraft who interprets signals, identifies targets and threats, and tells the pilot when to fire weapons. The EWO also acts as a spotter in identifying enemy planes.

Geneva Conventions International treaties and protocols designed to protect noncombatants in war, specifically civilians, medical and religious personnel, the sick and wounded, and prisoners. The Third Geneva Convention requires that POWs be treated humanely and receive adequate food, shelter, and medical care and that camps be inspected by international organizations like the Red Cross.

Hoa Lo Prison The main prison in the city of Hanoi, where captured American aviators were locked up, beaten, and tortured. To the prisoners it was sarcastically referred to as the Hanoi Hilton.

MiG Soviet-made fighter aircraft. The North Vietnamese air force primarily used the MiG-21, which was as fast as American jets and more maneuverable. The name MiG comes from the last names of Soviet aircraft designers Artem Mikoyan and Mikhail Gurevich, with *i* being the Russian word for *and*.

Operation Rolling Thunder A sustained bombing campaign against North Vietnam that ran from March 2, 1965, to November 1, 1968.

pipper The very center of the gunsight on a fighter's gunnery platform, used by pilots when flying combat missions to aim their guns at enemy aircraft.

SAMs Surface-to-air missiles

SERE or **survival, evasion, resistance, and escape** Training that teaches service members to withstand interrogation and capture and to learn survival and escape techniques if they are captured by enemy forces.

Soviet Union A union of socialist republics that succeeded the Russian empire in the early twentieth century. Its fifteen republics encompassed much of Eastern Europe. During the Cold War, the United States and the Soviet Union were the two world superpowers. The Soviet Union provided weapons and military assistance to North Vietnam during the war.

Thud Nickname given to the F-105 Thunderchief by its pilots. Designed as a supersonic bomber, it was fast but not very nimble in aerial combat against enemy fighter planes.

Wild Weasels The nickname for the men who flew missions to destroy antiaircraft and SAM sites. Also used for the specially equipped two-seat F-105F Thunderchiefs, the name comes from the ferocious small animal that will go to any length to attack its prey.

NOTES

4 "and then at the last second": Leo K. Thorsness, interview, 2002, pt. 1, Veterans History Project, American Folklife Center, Library of Congress. memory.loc.gov/diglib/vhp-stories/loc.natlib.afc2001001 .89790.

4 "We would go in high": Ruhl, "Rendezvous," 1974.

7 "It was unwieldy": Thorsness, *Surviving Hell*, p. 1.

9 "the greatest concentration": Associated Press, "N. Viet Guns Tied to Rising U.S. Air Toll," *Chicago Tribune*, May 21, 1967.

16 "When I went to Vietnam": This and following quote are from Thorsness interview, Library of Congress. Edited for clarity.

20 "we defeated the Depression": Thorsness, *Surviving Hell*, pp. 15–16.

21 "hard and itchy work": Thorsness, p. 15.

22 "was serving without distinction": Thorsness, p. 17.

24 "he nearly squeezed": Ruhl, "Rendezvous," 1974.

31 "Kingfish lead": Thorsness, *Surviving Hell*, p. 3.

32 "I have both chutes": This and the following quote are from "Wild Weasel mission 19 April 1967," audio recording and transcript, posted by Plumalley, Wikisource, last updated April 16, 2016, en .wikisource.org/wiki/Wild_Weasel_mission_19_April_1967.

33 "It appeared the MiG": This and following quote are from Davis, *Wild Weasel*, p. 141.

35 "Brigham Control": The following radio conversation is from Thorsness, *Surviving Hell*, pp. 4–5.

41 "When the day for my first flight": Thorsness, p. 19.

43 "We slept in concrete bunkers": Thorsness, pp. 20–21.

44 "most nights I stayed up": Thorsness, p. 21.

44 "And, by the way": Thorsness, p. 21.

47 "Sandy One, Kingfish Lead": This and following quotes in chapters six and seven are from Thorsness, *Surviving Hell*, pp. 5–8.

59 "Cadillac here": Thorsness, p. 10.

59 "This is Carbine Three": Broughton, *Thud Ridge*, p. 148.

60 "My helmet ripped off": Unless otherwise noted, this and following quotes in chapters eight, ten, and eleven are from Thorsness, *Surviving Hell*, pp. 11–31.

89 "Gaylee": Thorsness, *Surviving Hell*, p. 120.

90 "Why me?": Leo Thorsness, "MOH Recipient Leo K. Thorsness Interview," June 13, 2007, Pritzker Military Museum and Library video, 1:09 mins., youtu.be/CBDJgyDCQaU.

91 "Well, I would hope": Thorsness interview, Library of Congress. Edited for clarity.

SELECTED BIBLIOGRAPHY

Boyne, Walter J. "Route Pack 6." *Air Force Magazine* 82, no. 11 (Nov. 1999). airforcemag.com/MagazineArchive/Pages/1999/November%201999/1199pack.aspx.

Broughton, Jack. *Thud Ridge*. Philadelphia: J. P. Lippincott, 1969. This thorough history of the Thud campaigns over North Vietnam does an excellent job of providing context on the decisions made in fighting an air war.

Carroll, Ward. "SERE School Is About More Than Just Being Tortured." We Are the Mighty. Dec. 22, 2014, wearethemighty.com/articles/sere-school-just-tortured.

Cugini, John D. "Republic Aircraft's F-105 Thunderchief." *Vietnam*, June 12, 2006. historynet.com/republic-aircrafts-f-105-thunderchief.htm.

Davis, Larry. *Wild Weasel: The SAM Suppression Story*. Carrollton, Texas: Squadron/Signal, 1986. An in-depth look at how the fight was taken to the SAM sites from the skies of North Vietnam.

DeLong, Kent. *War Heroes: True Stories of Congressional Medal of Honor Recipients*. Westport, Conn.: Praeger, 1993.

Frisbee, John L. "Wild, Wild Weasel." *Air Force Magazine* 68, no. 4 (April 1985). airforcemag.com/MagazineArchive/Documents/1985/April%201985/0485valor.pdf.

Hampton, Dan. *The Hunter Killers: The Extraordinary Story of the First Wild Weasels, the Band of Maverick Aviators Who Flew the Most Dangerous Missions of the Vietnam War*. New York: William Morrow, 2015. Highly readable, it gives a thorough examination of the strategy and tactics of the air war in Vietnam, especially in the early days.

Laurence, Mike [pseud.]. "The Thud." Vietnam Veterans Oral History and Folklore Project. Buffalo State College. Jan. 7, 1994. faculty .buffalostate.edu/fishlm/folksongs/thud.htm.

"Leo Thorsness." Online supplement to *American Valor*, directed by Norman S. Powell. PBS. 2003. pbs.org/weta/americanvalor/stories /thorsness.html.

Michel, Marshall L., III. *Clashes: Air Combat over North Vietnam 1965–1972.* Annapolis, MD: Naval Institute Press, 1997.

Ruhl, Robert K. "Rendezvous with the Rattlesnake." *Airman*, Dec. 1974. web.archive.org/web/20090803173147/geocities.com/Pentagon /7002/thorsnes.html.

Thorsness, Leo. *Surviving Hell: A POW's Journey*. New York: Encounter Books, 2008. Leo Thorsness's poignant autobiography deals extensively with his time as a prisoner of war in North Vietnam.

"Thud: The F-105 Thunderchief." Written and produced by Luke Swann, 1989. *Great Planes,* Discovery Channel. This excellent documentary covers the design, development, and deployment of the F-105 Thunderchief aircraft.